Best regards,
Alvis Howard
December 5, 1989

THE WINDS FROM HEAVEN

A PANSOPHY FOR THE TWENTY-FIRST CENTURY

ALVIS HOWARD

Honeysuckle Imprint
P.O. BOX 793 • HUNTSVILLE, AL 35804

Dedication

To all the people I have ever known who all have contributed something to this book.

THE WINDS FROM HEAVEN
A Honeysuckle Imprint Book/November 1989

Library of Congress Catalog Card Number: **89-080891**
ISBN: **0-9621455-2-1**

TYPOGRAPHY BY BPS STUDIO

PRINTED IN THE UNITED STATES OF AMERICA

CONTENTS

PROLOGUE

> ***At that time this people and Jerusalem will be told, "A scorching wind from the barren heights in the desert blows toward my people, but not to winnow or cleanse; a wind too strong for that comes at my command. Now I pronounce my judgment against them.***
>
> ***Jeremiah 4:11***

There is always a critical moment in time when an act is committed from which future events are determined. Military officers, who study the great battles of history, are most aware of this. Historians too, search always for such pivotal and critical acts. At one moment in the Sixties, a homosexual in Haiti randomly chose a sexual partner who carried in his African genes a deadly pestilence. There in that lush grotto of the Caribbean, that had become a haven for homosexual liaisons, an act was committed that set in motion a death reaper whose sickle is gleaning the entire earth.

In 1949, Robert Vogler, a vice president with the ITT Corporation, was arrested in Hungary and falsely charged with spying. Up until that time, innocent Americans believed that they could expect protection from their government, that the government would actually go to war if necessary to secure the release of even one American. Because of this, Americans roamed the world with feelings of security and safety, believing that they were safe anywhere in the world. But, when the American government appeared impotent and failed to gain the release of Vogler, and merely blabbered and huffed and puffed, it was an act with momentous future consequences. It would culminate in the Iranian hostage crisis. Americans went in three short decades, from feeling safe anywhere in the world to feeling unsafe everywhere in the world.

There are thousands upon thousands of people living on the streets of America today who were, just a few short years ago, dancing through fields of wild flowers playing on flutes. Love then floated about on everyone's lips like beads of water on an oily surface. But, it was loved imagined, rather than love with foundation. It was like trying to put bones in cotton candy. It was a sad and fragile era.

What followed was bitterness and hate. A war grounded in a clash of cultures tore the fabric from a society that had never known defeat. One culture measured success and time in infinity while the other was frenzied if success took longer than a few months. The outcome and the victor, taking patience into consideration, was never really in doubt. The Gods have always taught that to have patients is to have anything. Government spirits internalized themselves and political reality turned to bile. A president was toppled from office and slunk away to the seaside to peer out to sea like Napoleon on Elba.

Great institutions forever lost the people's confidence and had dignity stripped to shreds. Ink and electronic tradesmen came to feed the insatiable appetite of a people who were now dependent on an ever increasing diet of personal scandal and shame. Once the underbelly of power was exposed to reveal that power was worthless unless it had a monetary value attached to it; a now jaded populace quickly moved to the terminal stage of civilization — greed.

The winds from heaven are sweeping the earth. There is a new spring on the way. Winter will come first.

PREFACE

There are those who deny truth when it would replace a generally accepted perception. This is always the case when the perception is actually true.

A spiritual being was planted on earth by a seed carried by a divine star set in motion by a heavenly wind. This spiritual being grew to maturity and mated with a daughter of earthly beings who were void of any spirit. The humans that grew from the seed of the divine star defied a heavenly mandate when they joined their spirits with the bodies of the daughters of the earth. From that moment on, humans walked the earth both as spirit and earth.

The body is the most perfect organism in the universe. It has been sculptured from stardust and imaged by a heavenly wind. The spirit is eternal and is malleable. It can be nourished into an image of light or darkness. Its immuned to any pain except that which is self-inflicted.

Souls are arcs that can seek light or darkness. The path of light is extremely narrow and is eternal. The path of darkness is vast and limitless. A hundred billion stars of a galaxy can collapse into a black hole so condensed its the size of a particle of an atom. The heat within these dark holes is immense. The universe is pocked with these compacted hells. There is no greater outer darkness.

The winds move silently and eternally over all the earth and throughout the universe. The wind is hauntingly beautiful when it gently massages the body in the morning, gliding off a mountain lake or open sea. Its fragile and delicate in the late afternoon puffing curtains and causing them to sway. It comes in fury and destruction as whirling, dancing tornadoes or savage and brutal, relentless hurricanes and typhoons. Over time, nothing cleanses like the wind. Job said, "Now no one can look at the sun, bright as it is in the skies, after the wind has swept them clean."

The earth and its inhabitants have become a huge boil that is festering critically, it is desperately in need of lancing. It has reached the point that it is poisoning the entire system of the planet and is spreading into the heavens. This poison must be allowed to drain and the wound exposed to pure air and light to heal cleanly. There is only one physician that has the skill to do this. ***A heavenly wind is coming as a lance.***

Alvis Howard

Huntsville, Alabama
September 1989

LIFE

Humans deal with life as children with their play, Who first misuse, then cast their toys away.

William Cowper

The universe is a perfect ecosystem. It all works perfectly. Nothing is left to chance. What it needs, when it needs it, how much it needs, it produces. Nothing whatsoever disturbs its motion. In recent time, nuclear materials and other toxicants have entered into space in amounts that are causing momentary cosmic pollution. These pollutants will be neutralized and a normal balance resumed as sure as the sun rises and sets.

The universe is a perfect system. As it dies, it is instantly reborn again. All the tiny matter that makes up the universe never dies, it is forever being created and forever being recreated. The universe, within human knowledge, is only one of endless universes. Many wonder what is outside the universe or is there an end or boundaries to it. The answer is that its like the remark made by a cynical wit in the Thirties, about a city that had earned her contempt, "There is no there, there!" This is the only way the universe could work. There can be no limit to expansion; because if there is a limit, then there is an end. Universes end but are instantly reborn and begin anew. It is all so magnificent.

There are empty voids instantly being created to accommodate expansion. Its like air flowing into a balloon, the more air that goes in, the larger the balloon becomes. When the air is released the balloon collapses. Outside the balloon there is unlimited space for it to expand. There could never be enough balloons to fill the available space, especially since there would be as many losing air as there would be gaining air or collapsing. That's the way the universe works.

People are not unlike universes; people are forever dying and forever being reborn. Each piece of matter that forms a person, is eternal. It not only never perishes; it never deteriorates. It is eternally pristine. It dissolves from one shape or state to another instantly. There is no extinction in the cosmos.

A beautiful reality of the earth is that there is no discrimination. The sun does shine equally on all. Material circumstances vary widely throughout the earth, but this variance in people values, is people related, not externally related to any inequality of the cosmos. There are many variations in land upon the earth, both good and bad, but no matter what condition any spot of land may be at any given time, it was once and many times, a fertile spot. Everything has its time and season. The nature of beings that have finite forms, is to try and relate almost everything to a nonexisting, element-reality in the universe — time and distance. There are no time and distances reality as from *now to then* or *from here to there*. The only reality in the cosmos is motion. Nothing stands still. The universe is a busy place. Nothing is standing still and there is no idle position. Its an active environment so dynamic that it takes away the breath!

Life cannot stand still either. From the moment of birth, life really takes on the characteristic of free falling from a high cliff. The outcome is inevitable in that the falling will come to an abrupt stop eventually. What makes this analogy applicable is that nothing — screaming, kicking, flailing against the winds, etc. — can halt the descend. Once off the cliff and on the way down there is no way back. Life is motion. The way to have the smoothest journey is to imitate a race car by getting into a heavenly draft whose motion and direction is sure.

The wonder of life is that there is a heavenly draft that draws everything along. Problems only occur when there is resistance to this draft. Birds migrate thousands and thousands of miles, generation after generation, trusting to a heavenly draft. Gossamer spiders sail aloft on the winds of a heavenly draft across oceans at heights of more than 50,000 feet. Bees travel inerrantly miles from a hive to transport nectar trusting in a heavenly draft. The birds of the air, the beast of the fields, and the fish beneath the sea, over millions of years, have moved in the motion of a heavenly draft, secure of an arrival at a final destination.

A prophet once said, "Behold the lily of the valley, they toil not nor do they reap, but I tell you King Solomon in all his glory was not arrayed as one of them."

To trust in a heavenly draft requires faith and faith requires truth and truth requires wisdom. Microscopic science has reached the point that protein structures have been photographed with amazing definition to the point that they may possibly be duplicated by chemical means using the photograph as blueprints. But, as has been learned in dissecting the atom, the deeper inside the atom you go, and the smaller the particle becomes, there always seems to be smaller ones still; a quark here and another quark there. What will ultimately be found is that there is no smallest, just as there is no largest. To limit size is like limiting the universe, if you limit it, it disappears. So like the universe — at the point the subatomic particles disappears, it is instantly recreated. All individual matter is an embryonic universe. This alone provides a staggering idea of the number of universes there are.

Imagine two pyramids with one pyramid atop the other touching at their smaller end — the end that is sharp and comes to a point. That is how the universe works. It expands out to a point and at the point it disappears it is recreated and begins growing again.

How does this relate to truth. Truth is like an atom, there are truths, subtruths, and subsubtruths. Truth is also like the universe in that at the point it appears to disappear, it is instantly born again. Truth is also like life in that once it is put in motion it continues on like a weight falling through the air. Once truth has leaped off of the cliff — hiding, denying, flailing against the wind, screaming, howling, etc. — nothing can ever stop its motion as it free falls through aeon after aeon of time. Truth is a reality perceived on different levels by different people at different times. Reality is the real point here because *only truth can have a reality. A lie has only an imaginary form; it has no real shape or being*. Once a man who had been blind from birth had his sight restored by a passing stranger. The blind man, who had his sight restored, was asked by many who and what the stranger was. The blind man always replied, "All I know is that once I was blind and now I see." That was his reality.

It is the unending levels of truth that confuse many. Reality or truth must be personally perceived. This was best demonstrated by a famous prophet who was once asked, "What is truth?" His nonanswer of the question provided the best possible answer. No one can tell someone else what the truth is. You can tell someone what you believe is the truth and unless they perceive it that way themselves, it will not be the truth for them. Truth can only be demonstrated on one level, the level right at the point where it is about to disappear and be reborn again. Because it is at that level that it has achieved its most universal reality. This is the level that truth achieves spirituality and it is also at this level that religious truths are born. *Truth, like steel and words, must be tempered to achieve its maximum edge.*

It is only with the application of truth that truth can have any value. The gossamer spider applies the truth by casting off into the heavenly draft with sublime confidence to sail along thousands of miles in the winds from heaven. Winds that cannot be seen nor whose duration can ever be determined. Of course, a logical dialogue that usually arises relative to these kinds of analogies is that the lower animals cannot think and if they could, they would have a lot of questions and doubts about their situations too. Which raises another point about another truth, or the truthful answer to a dynamic question: Is it better to think or not to think and is man the only animal that thinks? To the second question first. To make decisions requires thought or what we call thought. To this extent, all animals think. The real difference is choice. So, the question is, is man the only animal that has a choice in the decision making process? Again, based on the premise that to make decisions requires thought, and since all animals can choose to eat or drink or not eat or drink, to go in one direction or another direction, they have a choice. The difference is in the number of choices. Animals choices are mechanical, limited to a yes, no, left, right, etc. Humans have as many choices as the imagination can contrive. Therein lies the problem. A prophet once said, "Come to me hot or cold, for if you come to me lukewarm I would spew you out of my mouth. For a double-minded human is unstable in all things."

In the movie *Black Sunday,* an agent of the Israeli intelligence service, Mosad, was stabbed to the point of death by a member of the Palestine Liberation Organization. The agent's younger partner was visiting him in the hospital and the older agent, who had been stabbed, was talking rather sadly about all of the killings on both sides. The younger agent told him rather cogently, "You are beginning to see both sides of the question and that can be very dangerous!"

It is the single-minded nature of all life, save humans, that allows a total faith in the winds from heaven that provide a heavenly draft to sail along in the perpetual motion of the universe. Forever humans have been reluctant actors in the grand theatre of life. They have never trusted either the script or the director. They have always felt that they knew words that would improve and enlarge their lines and certainly had more experience than the director in acting upon their earthly stage. They have constantly, over thousands of years, tried to enlarge and expand their parts, in this eternal play. This bickering between actors and director have not always been one sided. There was the Tower of Babel. Here the actors were all speaking in one voice and were playing their parts to the hilt. However, the director became concerned that at the rate the actors were going they would be able to do anything, even the things that the director could do. So, the director gave all of the actors new and different lines and they became very confused went off in different directions and have never regained any degree of harmony since.

It is a rather strange paradox that on the one hand it would appear that the major problem is that humans are the only animals that are always going off in ten different directions, appearing never to know what's ahead. On the other hand when they were living single-mindedly, the director stepped in and deliberately changed their lines. It was done to confuse them and everyone else so that they would not work together. The fear was that they would then be on the same level as the director. Then there is the admonition that everyone should be single-minded.

Actually, both ideas are the same and both ideas are right. Perception has always been more acceptable than reality. Gods, kings, prophets, politicians, artists, merchants, etc. have always known that the easiest way to achieve a coveted end or provide a solution to a vexing problem was to suspend reality and weave a perception that was in accord with the prevailing, overwhelming, populace's desire. Over the ages manipulators of human events have raised the development of artificial perception to a very high art form.

If faith is the substance of things hoped for, but the realization of things not seen, artificial perception is the substance of things seen, with the reality of things not hoped for.

Image— the cosmetic stardust of the mind. Humans are said to be made in the image of the creator, a comparison not too flattering; an image is an imitation. Not being the real thing always suffers in comparison. It may be a balm to say that imitation is the sincerest form of flattery; but it is also, unfortunately, a sadness that flattery is insincere praise. Humans are an imitation wrapped in an insincerity. Nothing is original with humans. No wonder they are so unhappy. All they do pales in comparison with all else. Imitators and imitations suffer a fatal flaw. They are and can never be real until there is a change in both form and content. Thus, all great philosophies and religions embody a rebirth. A human seeking knowledge of this once went in darkness to speak with a controversial prophet. "What would I have to do to obtain the status you say I need to reach to be happy?" "To obtain the grace I speak of, you must be born again," the prophet answered.

"But, how can I be born again? I cannot enter into my

mother's womb a second time!" The human seeking knowledge asked, very puzzled.

"I've tried to explain earthly things to you and obviously you are not understanding what I'm saying. So, how could you understand if I try to explain heavenly things to you." The prophet said and then added, "The wind comes and the wind goes. No one knows where it comes from or where it goes."

The winds from heaven that gently blows a new spirit into the vain flesh of humans, is constantly in motion across the earth and throughout the universe. To receive the spirit requires moving out of the darkness of fear into the light of faith. *For the winds of heaven carry not the spirit of fear, but love, power, and a sound mind!*

There is no magic trick ever conceived by a conjurer, no matter how amazing or complex in form or illusion, that is not extremely simple in execution. The more complex the illusion, the more simple the execution. Life is a form of trillions of amazing illusions. This is why the young understand best the things perceived but not seen. The simple things of the world do truly confound the wise; and the wise things of the world are truly understood by the simple.

To humans who needs all the reinforcement possible and their egos constantly fueled to continue any race, nothing is more anathema than to view an endeavor as anything less than complex and monumental. To do so is at minimum, high heresy. To human's fragile countenance a simple solution is no solution. This is why humans find few, if any, real or long term solutions to so many human derived problems.

Henry David Thoreau once said, "I have often seen people hacking away at branches, but I never see anyone chopping away at the roots."

Experts of all stripes say that drugs are the most complex and unsolvable problem facing humanity. They indicate that it is a 100 billion dollar a year industry and much of it is fed by crime.

Other experts say that thieves and robbers steal and rob 50 billion dollars a year to get drugs. They also say that thieves can only get a fraction (from one-tenth to one-hundredth) of the actual value of the items they steal when they sell them. If the thieves can only get one-tenth of the value of the items they steal that means they are stealing one trillion dollars worth of items a year. There are not that many televisions, watches, and VCR's in America.

There is also no 100 billion dollars a year in the ghettos of the major cities of America. Ninety percent of the drug money comes from judges, lawyers, singers, actors, writers, car dealers, real estate brokers, television anchors, stock brokers, doctors, dentists, etc. The drug trade is fueled by money; cut off the money, cut off the drugs.

Start arresting lawyers, judges, singers, actors, writers, car dealers, real estate brokers, television anchors, stock brokers, doctors, dentists, etc. Confiscate their BMW's, condos, sailboats, and ski chalets. Mete them the same justice as ghetto inhabitants, and drugs in America will be history.

WHY? WHY? WHY? Like little children humans forever cried, "Why?" The really big WHY is WHY ARE WE HERE? (Here being here on earth alive). Humans are an important factor in the universe. Everything is important in the universe. But, humans are important above all else — for a purpose.

If a tree falls in a forest where no one is there to hear it fall, does the fall make a sound? Yes. But, the sound has no meaning because unless an action or a thing is perceived, it has no form or expression. Its a void.

Humans the imitators, imitate their creator to the extent

that this magnificent, jigsaw, puzzle universe, can be put together in as many shapes and forms as there are imaginations. Only one will fit all of the pieces properly. When the puzzle is solved, humans will come together again as one with God and the pieces will be jumbled all over and tossed out on the empty and unlimited spaces and it will start all over. The players will be the same, but the puzzle will be completely new.

Alcohol and drugs bend the mind and accelerate the ability to fantasize. No right solution can be found in an altered state of mental comprehension. Its one of the illusions of the cosmetic stardust of the mind. Its a perception that is totally void of reality.

Sin is not doing right. Few people do right so under that definition, there is a lot of sin. But sin is not bad to everyone. One human's sin, is another human's pleasure. Gods normally don't enjoy sin. Most Gods find sin among the really vexing characteristics of humans. The more human humans are, the more sinful they are. Which would explain why Gods would be offended by sin. The catalog of sin is very, very long. Little that humans do is not sin. Taking motivation and reason into consideration, everything is sinful. But nothing is sinful in itself. It's the English that is put on sin that causes it either to go into the right pocket or to muck about the table making another shot by anyone else practically impossible.

Sin is either a misdeed or an act against the will or tenets of God. There is no act or thought in life that is a sin in and of itself. There is no act or thought in life that is not a sin.Contradictory? No! A fire has many beneficial effects; it is also very dangerous and destructive. It depends upon how something is used. When it is said, *"All sin."* This is a true statement. It is a statement that repels many. Even for those who do not believe in sin, every human act (and sin is a human act) results in either a good effect or a bad effect. This is such a simple fact of life that not to understand it would place one in the category of an idiot. This is a cornerstone of understanding since all discipline hinges on this fact. For unless everyone is equally sinful and the only way this could be true is for all things to be sinful, then there would be an easy way out for many who claim exemption from sin by lack of access to the means for sinning.

No sin or act is without consequences.

The great unifying cry in the Seventies and early Eighties was, "It doesn't harm anyone else what consenting adults do in the privacy of their homes." The Government (via taxes) may well spend a trillion dollars before AIDS is curbed, if it ever is. In one way or another, everyone is effected by everything everybody does — consenting or unconsenting.

It is an irony that many who fear death the most are also the ones who despair life the most. Robert Louis Stevenson, the author of *Treasure Island*, once said with remarkable insight, "If you love life, you will also love death, for the author of the former is also the author of the latter." The logical question arises, If death is so wonderful, why go through the pains and worries of life? Why not just do away with life and have only an afterlife? The answers are simple. One, there could be no afterlife without there first being a life. There is also a reason for living; its to prepare for death. Its akin to the age old problem, you can't be a carpenter unless you belong to the union and can't belong to the union unless you are a carpenter. Of course one becomes a carpenter by beginning as a helper, then a learner, then an apprentice, then a novice, then a junior, then a senior, and finally a master carpenter. Its the same in life, if you want to be happy in death you have to learn to be happy in life.

Because:

THERE IS NOTHING IN HEAVEN NOR ON EARTH THAT CAN MAKE ANYONE HAPPY — NOT RICHES, NOT FAME, NOT POWER, NOT LOVE, NOT BEAUTY — THERE IS ABSOLUTELY NOTHING EXTERNALLY THAT CAN BRING HAPPINESS. HAPPINESS IS AN INTERNAL STATE THAT RESULTS IN HAPPINESS REGARDLESS OF ALL EXTERNAL STIMULUS.

The two decades from the Sixties to the Eighties have shown that rich, beautiful, famous people can be the saddest, unhappiest, miserable humans alive. From Marilyn Monroe to Elvis Presley and from President John F. Kennedy to Liberace, sex, power, drugs, and wealth were not enough in the end to save them. To the greedy, enough is never enough.

The beginning of happiness has only one source, the acceptance of responsibility for ones own acts. This begins all growth.

To live the best life, one needs to begin as a helper and progress to a master. Because only a master can sail in the winds from heaven. The alternative is to sink into the vortex of space where there in no direction. *No matter what you believe in life or whether you believe anything at all, there is one absolute certainty, you will either sail upon the winds from heaven or disappear in a vortex of space.*

The certainty in this is that there is an alternative to everything: there cannot be a black without a white, a wet without a dry, a cold without a hot, and there cannot be a good without a bad. Therefore, there is a good afterlife and a bad afterlife. Just as there is a good life and a bad life. No one can accept responsibility for their own actions until they accept this. For there would be no need for responsibility unless there were good, bad, or better alternatives for everything that is done. Responsibility involves acting responsibly. Responsibility is a burden. It can be a heavy burden or a light burden, but responsibility is a burden. The wonderful thing about a burden is the wonderful feeling that is felt when it is lifted. Thus the heavier the burden the greater the feeling. The most impoverished soul in the universe is the one without a burden of any kind.

It must be remembered that the responsibility and burden that is being discussed here is personal responsibility. Not professional responsibility, job responsibility, or civic responsibility. If an individual accepts personal responsibility, they will always display the right kind of responsibility in all other areas.

An oft thought of question is: since there are so many different people of so many different races scattered over so much of the earth, an earth that is so different in so many places; how can one set of ideas apply when they all are so different? A perceived truth in New York is the same in Mwanza, Kenya; or Ulan Bator, Mongolia; *if it is perceived the same.* Broad cultural and environmental conditions provide broad differences in perception. At the roots, salt is salty and sugar is sweet, the world over. The major differences is in the availability and the use of these items. Salt and sugar are exotic luxuries in some places and just ordinary common place things elsewhere. At the very atomic sublevel of all existence is one shared trait from which flows all truth and all reality and that is RESPECT.

When the gods would bestow gifts, they require first and foremost complete respect. From ancient gorges of Africa to the cliff top haciendas of Santa Barbara, California, its respect that always sought. Not only do we need respect personally, but we must have something or someone externally to respect.

Because respect stems from a reflection of or mirror image of the values we covet.

No one can respect anyone or anything anymore than

they respect themselves.

The most awful appellation that can be applied to anyone, because it strikes to the very heart of character, is that someone has no self-respect.

The greatest accolade that can be given anyone is to respect them. If the respect is out of love. The worse accolade is to respect someone out of fear.

Royalty once demanded respect out of fear. The only significant royalty left remains because of respect out of love.

Life is not complex. If it were, there would not be any ordinary people. There are more ordinary people than there are extraordinary people. There are more ordinary people who have done extraordinary things than there are extraordinary people who have done any better than ordinary.

Its the mind junk, fostered by a cartoon concept of reality, creating a montage of Salvador Dalian dimensions, that is causing so much mental flameout. Music that destroys hearing, clothes that in earlier times were sold as workshop cleanup rags, food that is so adulterated that pictures have to be used on the packaging to identify it, movies and television shows that make stupidity a national virtue, and political leaders so void of character and honor that symbols such as Christmas Trees and Flags are used to sell them to a paisley population. Heroes are not heroes just because the public says they are.

Abraham Lincoln once got up to follow a man who had just made an extremely long-winded speech. Lincoln asked the crowd, "If you count a horses' tail as a leg, how many legs would he have."

"Five!" The crowd responded in unison.

"Not so.' mused Lincoln, "Calling a horses tail a leg,

does not make it one."

What is sometime perceived as complex really is based on a simple theory. The radar Doppler effect, developed during World War II, was like that. The principle was that the noise of something going away, like a train, got fainter the farther away it got. Contrastly, in the opposite direction, if a train was approaching, the closer it got the louder the noise would get. That's all the radar did. It would send out a beam and if it hit an approaching object, the faster the beam came back, the closer the object was. The longer it took the beam to return, the farther away the object was getting. As we move forward, the past recedes and eventually fades from memory. It is still there. As we move forward there is constantly something new and wonderful up ahead. There is something up ahead forever. What is behind is also there forever. The present, the past and the future are always there at the same time.

There is in the universe genes that compose all humans a structure that works best in harmony with all other particles. It is when we are in tune with that basic structure that we are the most healthy and happiest. It is when we are out of tune with that structure that we are the most unhappiest and the unhealthiest. Few words are every very adequate to accurately convey precisely what is intended, especially when discussing things universal. "Spiritual" or "religious" are probably the best words to describe how one can best be in harmony with this universal basic structure. Ancient people who were more in tune with the universe than modern people, sensed this deep and abiding law. They knew that regardless of all other forces, it was this strange and mystic innerforce that most often governed an ultimately determined the course of their lives. They also knew that to be in harmony with this force provided inner peace and to be out of harmony with it meant turmoil and agony. Many modern practitioners of mental science place this in the realm of myth and ignorance. Witch doctors and priests did motivate and maintain their positions through installation of such fears. There is ample evidence that even at the beginning of time, earliest humans, sensed some inner force that tugged for and responded to nourishment by way of mental reflection and reverence. There is in humans a need to respond to this inner force. Most of the ills of the world, both physical and mental, are a direct or indirect results of ignoring this most basic of all human needs.

The mind, spirit and soul never ages. They are as pristine when you are 105 as they are when you are born. The reason it does not appear so to so many, is that the mind, spirit, and soul are the least used of human elements. If the mind, spirit, and soul could collect mental cholesterol, ninety percent of the human race would be dead before they were eighteen. The mind, spirit, and soul, like the physical part, if not used, gets and remains flaccid. No human element needs or craves nourishment more than the mind, spirit, and soul, because they are so often neglected. It has been estimated that almost all humans die having used only a fraction of their brains, and only a minuscule portion of their mental capacity. The mind, spirit, and soul are the most valuable of human assets and the most wasted.

One of the great fears of all humans is lost of control; that feeling of helplessness. This is one of the reasons death holds such a fearful grip on most people. Its the feeling of helplessness; the feeling that you will die and there is nothing to stop it. You will disappear and be taken away, where, when, and how without you being able to do anything about it. That your mind, spirit, and soul will fade away like your body. But, the mind, spirit, and soul is eternal. It will not fade away. It will be as young and bright on the date of your death as it was on the date of your birth.

Textbook-intellectuals and cosellian philosophers reject this since the brain is a physical organ that has chemical and electron aspects that stores, sorts, and disperses information and data much like a computer. They conclude that there are no spiritual aspects to it at all. They fail to understand that computers are only systems and conveyances for processing information and data. The most complex computer conceived by humans is impotent until it has been programmed, or given artificial stimulance before it can add 2 and 2 to come up with the sum of 4.

The human fetus at conception is imprinted with more knowledge than all the computers in the world linked together could duplicate. At death, this knowledge is exactly as it was at conception. Knowledge allows humans to perform a variety of functions in a variety of ways. Humans cannot expand knowledge, but they can infinitely expand the use of that knowledge. All that exists, seen and unseen, is present now and forever.

Its interesting that almost every religion, philosophy, and order in the world, both modern and ancient, stresses the attainment of wisdom and expansion of knowledge. The reason for this is obvious. Every life form in the universe, including the universe itself, requires some form of nourishment to grow. Without exception, when this nourishment is withdrawn for a certain period of time, then that life form will perish, whether it be animal, vegetable, mineral, a star, or a black hole in space. Thus, the spirit, mind, and soul would also perish unless it receives the nourishment of thought.

Not just any thought.

Everything that exists has a definite and specific molecular structure that is codable and printable. Its like a jigsaw puzzle, the pieces can only go together one way. If you try to jam a piece into the wrong place, it will technically work to the extent that the space may be either partially filled or filled too much. It will not make the perfect image that it is suppose to make unless all of the right pieces are in the right places. That is exactly what happens with humans. Each human has a definite and specific molecular structure, codable and printable. A process for coding and printing this structure is not now available. It may be hundreds of years in the future before it is available. The spirit, mind, and soul is not codable and printable, and it never will be. The spirit, mind, and soul function most properly and harmoniously when the physical body is functioning according to its proper structure.

What is the proper nourishment to achieve this healthy and harmonious state?

There are two key elements.

The first element is moderation. This is so obvious because *moderation simply means the right amount*, not too much and not too little. Just like the jigsaw puzzle, the right amount in the right place.

The second element is love. The opposite of love is hate. *There are degrees of love and there are degrees of hate, but there are no alternatives to one or the other.* You will either, in a lesser or greater degree, depending on infinite factors, love or hate. This applies to people, knowledge, religion, God, clothes, food, home, country, self, life, etc. Depending on your choice of love or hate, you will nourish your spirit, mind, and soul with one or the other. Every time you nourish your spirit, mind, and soul with love, you're putting the right pieces in place. When you nourish your spirit, mind, and soul with hate, you're putting the wrong pieces into place.

No matter who you are on this planet or no matter what your circumstances or condition, age or sex, hate in any degree or form will not properly fit your spirit, mind, and soul. It will not ever, ever feel right.

This is not theory, religion, philosophy, or aimless uttering, *this is fact.* Its the simplest thing to prove. Everyone is capable of loving and hating. Its a matter of choice. It only has to be tried to see what feels the best.

The saddest thing in life is when anyone puts nothing but hate into their spirit, mind, and soul. Like a jigsaw puzzle with all the pieces in the wrong place, such a spirit becomes unrecognizable from its original image. It kills itself by becoming something totally different from its real self.

Be moderate and love and you will have the greatest possession that can be owned in this life — peace of mind.

On the scale of time, humans have been apportioned very little. Its difficult for the average human to live much beyond the age seventy. This is just a whiff of time. Its something that has been lamented throughout human existence. Attempts to assuage this brevity is made by religion, poetry, philosophy, and literature — everything except a reason. This is curious, because there is a reason for everything. Nothing happens in this universe without a reason and the reason always reveals that the way things happen is for the best.

Why have humans been allotted such small spans of existence?

It is paradoxical that humans, frail and imbued with little time, are composed of and surrounded by things eternal. To compound the issue, it is only to humans that time is of the least importance. Time is a friend of all but humans.

Great debates rage over the length of time it took for the universe to be created, when its of absolutely no value whatsoever to determine whether it took six days, six weeks, or six billion years. Time did not exist before this universe was created; it did not exist after it was created; and, beyond the human sense, it does not exist now, nor will it exist in the future. Time is a human equation that does not have an infinite reality within the context of the universe. Human life, is measured in human terms; not in any terms that is related to the universe. Even the time humans have created to define for their imaginations the distances within the universe such as a light year. A light year is the distance that light travels in a year. The distance is 5,878,000,000,000 miles. There are stars that are millions of light years away from earth. The magnitude of the universe, both in distances between various planets and stars and in lengths of time from conception to present, is so immense that few can comprehend it. It is hard to get the conscious mind to even accept this immensity. There is a tendency for the mind to shutter when trying to visualize this vastness. The human mind cannot swallow nor digest the universe. The human mind can nibble at small chunks or gnaw on the marrow, but the whole universe cannot be eaten by the mind.

The span of human life is reduced to insignificance in relationship to the immense mental statistics of the universe. It is the human mind that gives reality to all of this and strangely, the mirror that reflects this magnificence, is shattered almost before it can reflect anything. The value humans place on various things is usually directly proportional to the rarity or durability of the item, such as a diamond or gold. On this scale, time, in human terms, is the rarest of all commodities. If one could live the 969 years that Methuselah lived it would be but a pip of cosmic expanse.

Humans marvel at life forms that have what is considered brief life spans. Such as certain insects and sea creatures that may have life spans of mere hours or even less. In terms of cognizance, humans may have the briefest span of all. The brevity of life is a constant in human existence. Usually the constant is constant concern. Humans are the only life form in the universe that spend most of their existence over concern for how little time they have. All other life forms get on with accomplishing the purpose for which they are here. These life forms are conceived, born, mature, mate, die, all endlessly and as effortlessly as the surf washes a beach.

The problem lies with the word "purpose." Everything that is known seems to have a purpose that can be reasonably and logically concluded, except humans. Humans cannot seem to find a purpose that is satisfactory. Religion tries to explain it, and it satisfies many to a greater or lesser degree, but there are usually, if not always, lingering doubts. There are many who think it all accidental and that there is no purpose or meaning. Existentialists believe that it can never be adequately or logically explained. But the end result of everything in the universe is positive, not negative. Therefore, humans are a positive not a negative and therefore have a purpose. Thus, the brief amount of time that humans live is explainable.

Everything that has appeared in the universe did so because of need. What was needed was created. Both animals and plants have been given complex and ingenious defense and immune systems for protection against predators and diseases. The atmosphere of the earth is perfect for life. None of this is by accident. Even if there were no God, none of this could be termed an accident or a freak of nature. An accident is something that happens that was not suppose to happen and a freak is something that is unusual, usually one of a kind. Neither can possibly describe this perfect universe. Everything that happens,

happens because it is necessary and needed. One thing can not happen without the other and one thing can not exist without the other.

Humans live as long as they need to, no more or no less. The desperation to expand life has had little success. The experts and many others will be quick to point out that the life span of humans has more than doubled in the last hundred years and more people are living past seventy than ever before. Both statements may be true within a certain context and confinement. But, there are millions of more humans now than has ever existed before and the human population is expanding at a phenomenal rate. If this is taken into the equation along with the genocide in Cambodia, the systematic starvation in Sudan and Ethiopia, AIDS, cancer, and heart attack epidemics worldwide, then the reality is that the life span is lower than it ever has been.

Drugs, transplants, etc. prolong life, but in most cases its just living only. There is no correspondingly, equal extension of quality of life. If one is confined to a bland, strict diet; cannot actively travel and enjoy life, in its many and varied forms, and is really a prisoner of a "do this or die regimen," just what is being expanded? Nothing. The great prophet who said, "I have come that you might have life and have it more abundantly." wasn't speaking of living on a life support system.

The purpose and only purpose of humans is caretakers. Like a tree falling in the forest without anyone there to hear the noise, its not really relevant whether it makes a noise or not. If no one is there to hear it, then the noise has no purpose. All existence has existence with humans. Before God there was darkness and a great void. Since the birth of humans, humans have displayed on walls of caves and stone monuments the inherent inner need to create and give expression to the ruminations of the mind. Creation is an expression of a monumental mind. Humans are the penultimate of this creation.

Many who try to conceive all of this are lost in minutia. In looking at the world from an aspect of disease, death, wars, famine, crime, murders, drugs, alcohol, etc., it really is a mess. Its been this way for ten thousand years. Ten thousand years are but a pip on the cosmic expanse. Humans are not good caretakers in some respect and are excellent caretakers in others. They certainly have been mucking things up for thousands of years and don't seem to be getting much better as time goes by. It may seem that way. Tiny progress is being made as time goes by, and on the universal scale there is plenty of time. Whether its ten years, ten hundred years, or ten thousand years, sooner or later, humans will get it right. The universe is infinitely patient. Every human ill is a result of human errancy.

The most difficult thing for almost any human to assume is responsibility. This is most graphically demonstrated by the almost total aversion, the entire world over, to writing. Whether in school, in business, in academia, or in private life, one of, if not the most difficult of tasks, is to get anyone to commit anything to writing. The reason for this is very, very simple. If someone says something to one person or a thousand, there is always deniability. One can always say they were misunderstood or things were taken out of context. Without something being written, there is always doubt. Even when it is written, the writer often denies having written it, even when handwriting experts are there to verify the authorship. Over and above all of this, the one thing that is absolutely exposed in any personal writing, whether its a simple note, a long message, or a complete book manuscript, is a pretty complete analysis of an individual's education, background, experience, talent, creativity, prejudice, skill, and commitment. Nothing is more revealing than the written word.

To be responsible is to be accountable. To be accountable is to accept success and also to accept failure. Humans should understand that everything in the universe fails successively, but not ultimately. It is nothing to try and fail; it is everything to fail to try. The greatest of human successes over time has been perceived at the time as failures. Only the bridges of human events across chasms of time solidify into permanent successes and truths.

To live at all is to be responsible. Without responsibility there is no life. There can be no success without failure. One cannot achieve success or failure without being accountable for personal behavior and action. Good caretakers are always responsible and accountable. The more responsible they are the better the land they care for thrives. Where the caretaker is without responsibility, the land is barren and is good for nothing.

Land is made for growing things on, not for killing things on. When something is sown it grows and gives life. When something is killed it returns to the earth and does not grow again.

In the wild there is a survival of the fittest. Predators eat predators and all are predators in one manner or another. If the predators don't eat each other they eat the vegetation. Everything consumes and is consumed. Humans are the greatest predators of all. We eat animals, vegetables, and fruit. We breathe the air, drink the water, cut trees, mine coal and drill for oil and gas for fuel. Nothing is really safe from humans. No animal, plant, source of water, clean air, all are being ravaged indiscriminately by humans. The criminals in society go one step further, they prey on their own kind. They are the cannibals of society. As a class the criminal is beneath even the animals and other living forms. For animals and other life forms prey for food and survival, never out of hatred or laziness. Criminals have been outside the norm in every historical culture. They have been despised and punished with every conceivable heinous punishment, but still they thrive and still they increase.

The reason for this is simple — responsibility and accountability. In its purest view, criminals really can't lose. They don't want responsibility to start with, so if they are killed in committing a crime, they will never have to worry about responsibility. If they are successful, they gain what they need with no work, no worry, and no responsibility and no accountability. If they are caught and sent to jail or prison, they have the best of all worlds from their point of view. Not only do they have no responsibility and accountability, but they have someone else providing housing, clothing, food, medical care, and entertainment. They have all of the necessities of life without lifting one finger. Its really an appealing career if you are bent in the direction of avoiding responsibility. Almost every criminal that ever lived had a history from early age to death as having demonstrated a lack of interest in assuming normal responsibilities, whether in assuming a fair share of work at home, school work, father or mother responsibilities for children, jobs as adults, etc. They sought the easy way out. That humans have failed at curbing the growth of criminals at anytime in history is easy to understand. Punishment in the form of jailing is not punishment to someone who is looking for the easy way out, its really giving them exactly what they want.

Immediately there is the thought, "Why are they always trying to escape?" Simple. The criminal that tries to escape, is the criminal that has the greatest difficulty in accepting anyones rules but their own. The harder it is for a particular criminal to accept responsibility, even if its the responsibility of serving a certain amount of time behind bars, that will be the criminal who will go to any length to escape. There is nothing criminals want do to escape responsibility. To punish a criminal who had rather die than accept responsibility is almost impossible. Every criminal that has changed from being a criminal did so only after deciding to accept responsibility and accountability. There is really no other way.

All of this is at the core of life. Its really tragic that criminals and other irresponsible humans do not realize that it takes far more energy and effort to avoid responsibility and accountability than it does to accept it. Its even more tragic to understand that in the end, avoiding responsibility and accountability in reality is impossible. Responsibility and accountability is cumulative. It can be postponed, but it does not disappear. It just stacks up one on top of the other. Its as simple as running in a circle you always come back to the same place. The humans who start and continue to avoid responsibility all their lives, end their life as they started it, right back at the same place. ***They started out as a sieve and every chance they had during life to plug one of the holes in order to begin to add something to their life they avoided it. When they reached the end of life, they were still a sieve — empty. Every opportunity had passed right through them.***

BODY

These humans are blemishes at your love feasts, eating with you without the slightest qualm — shepherds who feed only themselves. They are clouds without rain, blown along by the wind; autumn trees, without fruit and uprooted — twice dead. They are wild waves of the sea, foaming up their shame, wandering stars, for whom blackest darkness has been reserved forever.

Jude 1:12-13

Supposing that we are made in God's image, then not only are we like God, but God is also like us. As we are constantly expanding our knowledge, God's knowledge is also expanding. Humans use only a tiny fraction of their mental capacity. In a lifetime, the vast majority of humans use less than ten percent. Geniuses use only about 40 percent. An analogy was once made that a computer that could do the things that an average human brain can do, would have to be so large that it would not fit into the Grand Canyon. On this scale, God possesses an awesome mental capacity. Humans possess huge mental capacities. Unfortunately, they're rarely used.

The mind is a lose cannon always in motion on a constantly rolling mental deck. It is almost impossible to harness and chain its constant curiosity and probing into things absurd, imaginative, unimaginative, and unimaginable. To discipline the mind, through the ability to concentrate for a few precious seconds on one object or subject, is a major, mental accomplishment. The mind has been succinctly described as like a white horse and a black horse constantly pulling against one another. Lord Byron said, *"Nor ear can hear nor tongue can tell the torture of that inward hell!"* But strangely enough, it is only with this unbridled kaleidoscopic configuration that a mind could function independently without external control. If it functioned methodically by some mathematical rote, then decisions would be mechanical, rather than extremporaneous, and thus subject to easy control. Given the propensity of humans to be lazy (just note the flabby body muscles) if the mind had not been put into perpetual motion, most brains would become atrophied before puberty. The magnificent thing about all of this is that no challenge on earth can equal the challenge of disciplining the mind not to bend in an ill wind or change capriciously to gain fair weather. The mind that is steady in a storm, will never yield to a dark temptation nor chart a crooked course. Unless you can control your mind, you can never control anything.

To understand life, you must first understand the law of opposites and objects. For everything in life there is an opposite or an object. For life there is death, for white there is black, for high there is low, for hot there is cold, and for man there is woman. Nothing can exist without an opposite, except the exception to the opposite law, which has the same end results. There are things that do not have an opposite but do have an object. Blood is an example. There is no opposite for blood, but human and animals are objects of blood. Without blood the object cannot exist. So the effect is the same as the opposite, without high there is no low, without blood there is no life, etc. It is essential to understand this since it provides a reasoned and logical rationale for many of the contentious emotional ideas of this era possessed by humans.

Of all the creatures in the universe, humans are the only creatures that have problems with sex. Humans are the only creatures in the universe who use sex not only for procreation but also try to use it for pleasure, with varying degrees of success. It is the pleasurable sex that causes the problems. Of all the natural functions in the universe, none are more natural than sex. In creating sex it had to be simple since the continuation of life depends on the accomplishment of sex. The problem with humans and sex is that humans put something into the sexual equation that no other species do. Humans put emotion into sex. Next to greed and ignorance, sex is the cause of more human deaths than anything else. Females of the species have been valuable bounty, next to land and gold, since the first two human creatures were created.

Sex is one of the fixations of the human mind. No society in the history of the planet have mused and fretted so much on body organs, functions, and performance as has the twentieth century. The words written on sex during the last thirty years would stretch to the very edge of the universe. If nothing else should dispel the idea of complexity, sex should. No human function is more gestated or more simple and universal than sex. It permeates life like and odor, seeping into every crevice of existence to the point in many cases so as to smother every other emotion and desire. The sad thing is that sex, like food, has been so adulterated, pictures and words have to be furnished to clarify and identify it. Sex has been imaged by manipulative pop culture merchants so that all products are endowed with a perceived, aphrodisiac quotient.

The reason for this human problem with sex is emotion, but it goes beyond that. In any sexual act, submission is required of one of the participating parties. If one party is submissive, then one party is dominate. Modernists claim that sexual acts should be among equals, that no one should be submissive and no one should be dominate. The problem is that if one is on top someone else and has a human body part inserted into that person, regardless of attitude or interpretation, one is submissive and one is dominate. Since it isn't a natural function to be submissive or dominate, these sexual roles cause feelings of guilt on the parts of both participants. Even in the case of parties who have a deep and abiding love for each other and the sexual act is consummated in the most tender way possible, there is a brief moment right after climax that is awkward. A feeling comes over both parties that they have just participated in something, the conclusion of which, should have had a feeling different than the one they have at that precise moment. All humans have this momentary feeling. Among humans that are very, very close it is extremely fleeting and is never contemplated beyond that moment. Among humans that are less than close or who are not on the best of terms or who are participating in a sexual liaison for reasons other than mutual, close love, these feelings can be dramatically severe and can cause awful mental acerbation.

There is a reason and good in this as there are reasons and good in everything.

The way human sexual relationships are formulated, neither party actually has a dominate or submissive role. It is this paradox that is revealing. The male of the species comes to the sexual role when there is a willing respondent, bearing a burden almost to large to carry. There is a sexual member that is difficult to control and acts more spontaneous than is ever desired. Regardless of these handicaps, there is the need to satisfy and the need to feel completely gratified. The male experiences sexual excitation on one level and one level only. This level can be reached in a sexual act with any female that results in climax. Males judge little difference between sexual partners.

The female has a thermal system that can only be controlled through certain physical and emotional stimulants; a thermal system that has a varying degree of receptivity at any given time and is erratic at best. The female requires the maximum stimulation of this thermal system at the period it is most receptive to achieving any significant sexual satisfaction. Females achieve sexual excitation in varying degrees, from slim pips to high peeks. A female may judge her sexual partner by the degree of excitation reached.

Sexual activity requires a tremendous amount of emotional energy for both the male and female. In the greatest sexual encounter that might be experienced, the actual length of the pleasure is mere moments. That such value is placed on such momentary excitation is another miracle of creation. That this momentary pleasure has such overpowering effects upon humans, insures the continued recreation of humanity.

There would be no problem with sex if humans did not use it for pleasure. If it were used only for procreation, there would not be a problem except for sterility. But, if sex did not carry a pleasurable aspect, there would be the possibility of far fewer births. There is also the personal warmth and spiritual ties that can be achieved between two humans when they share something as personal and intimate as sex. It is in this aspect of sex that submission and dominates has no bearing — *submission becomes an act of giving and dominance becomes an act of acceptance.*

Like many of the wonders of creation, there is nothing wrong with sex. It is a natural human function endowed with godly benefits when practiced with love. It can be awful and endowed with horror when practiced with hate.

Nothing provokes more emotion and less rationale. Humans spend more time between legs — both mentally and physically — than in any other human endeavor. This basic, human function, has been nuclearized into a mushroom cloud of obfuscation. Why? Principally to commercialize each fallout from the mushroom cloud. Sex is America's number one industry, internally and both as an import and export. Americans spend $22,000,000.00 each day on pornography alone.

Albert Camus, the French existentialist, once remarked, "I don't know if there is a God; but one thing I am sure of, if there is, he could care less what humans did with their puny sex organs."

God might or might not, but humans really need too. The opposite of man is woman and without woman there is no man. Two men alone cannot breed anything. Two women alone cannot breed anything. If there is no reproduction of a species, there is no species. What gets all fouled up in all of this is the mushroom cloud. Most humans don't really like the term "breeding." It sounds clinical and void of fun and excitement. But try as one might to change it, this is the original reason for the act. Having said that, it doesn't mean it cannot be fun, exciting, and lustful.

The magical cry was, and in many circles still is, *"Anything is all right between consenting adults."*

Think about that. Men and women, on drugs, on alcohol, and as clean as sunbleached sand, consent to many very interesting things. Medical personnel, in emergency wards and treatment centers, all over the world have had to medically removed almost every know object, that was thought to fit the form, size, and function, from every human orifice, front and back. Humans consent to being urinated and defecated upon. They consent to being beaten, chained, choked, pinched, and burned. On the scale of all human acts, all of these things probably are of minor importance to the overall picture of things, but to try to ascribe some kind of normality to them from an original human evolutionary standpoint is slightly ludicrous. Intellectuals do so with a giggle; others do so with stupidity.

Kinky sex could be best described as unusual or eccentric. The fact that it is given this connotation, even by those who practice it, take it out of the norm. The vast majority of those practicing kinky sex are middle-aged and older people with sexual dysfunctions or who need some thing highly erotic and bizarre for sexual arousal or to achieve some sort of sexual fantasy. All of the kinky scenarios such as dressing as a baby in diapers, dressing as all kinds of characters, may be innocent enough in most cases, certainly a little hilarious, depending on ones' sense of humor. But normal? Hardly.

Playing with yourself or masturbation might really be called the sex-of-choice of this generation. Its almost received the seal of approval from *Good Housekeeping*. Whether its right or wrong begs the point. The end results is the same as sucking on a popsickle stick. You can suck all day but the only thing you're going to get is the taste of wood and the imagination of what the popsickle might have tasted like. It is also rather humorous if you think about it. No one likes to be laughed at. Maybe its not humorous so much as great pathos. Here is a woman alone wreathing in bed vigorously rubbing her sexual part; here is a grown man sitting on his toilet commode, sweat drenched forehead, intensely viewing a magazine, frenziedly jerking his organ. Humans can't cherish this image of themselves. How we view ourselves accounts for how we feel.

Often advise columnists receive letters from wives and girlfriends inquiring about the normality of men dressing in women's clothes. This may be a harmless pursuit and if done in the privacy of one's home may harm no one. Maybe women's clothing are more comfortable than men's. But, a fifty year old, two-hundred and twenty-six pound truck driver cannot have a very proud image of himself as he rides down the highway thinking of how he looked the night before dressed in black bra and silk bikini briefs. As you think so are you.

The problem in sex comes when pederasts, child molesters, rapists, flashers, obscene telephone callers, etc., attempt sex with the unconsenting. The deaths, mutilations, and mental cauterizing that accompanies these violations are among the most sordid of all human acts. Nothing traumatizes a human more directly than does an involuntary sexual assault. Its a putrid, foreign penetration of human flesh that sears in such a way that often even time cannot cleanse completely. Even human slavery is not as awful as a sexual assault. Sexual aberrants have infested humanity since the beginning of civilization. At different moments in history, place, and time, many of these sexual aberrations have been condoned or even accepted as the norm of a particular society. Because of this, practitioners of these perversions find personal solace and an augur against critics. But the historical harvest, both ancient and modern, of these pseudo-heightened sexual practices has been bitter fruit. Bitter fruit that if it fell only in the orchards of these aberrants would have one significance, but the real horror is that this sexual fruit rots in all of society.

Thousands of individuals in universities, colleges, think-tanks, etc., ponder and spend millions and millions of dollars evaluating and rationalizing human sexual behavior. The reasons why and the blame for aberrant sexual appetites is really not the point. Its like spending millions of dollars on trying to determine if Humpty Dumpty fell off the wall or was pushed. What was important was that "...all the King's horses, and all the King's men, couldn't put Humpty together again." What is really important is this: Humpty Dumptys will always fall off walls or will be pushed and sexual aberrants will always leave broken victims in their wake. Better to spend the millions and millions of dollars on trying to find ways to put victims together again, if they survive. Its the innocent that really needs the care.

A nation that pretends world power whose national capitol is unsafe at any hour, is a nation in terminal trouble. If America could have a national day of mourning for the one characteristic that has suffered the greatest lost, America would have a national day of mourning for *Class.* Meaning class that has to do with style and verve. Once a nation of immense class and style, America is now a nation of trash.

In the movie *Patton*, General George Patton remarked to General Omar Bradley, concerning the defeat of American forces at Kasserine Pass, Tunisia, "Brad its as plain as the nose on your face. Any damn fool could see it. These guys don't look like soldiers, they don't act like soldiers and they sure as hell are not going to fight like soldiers!"

That's exactly America today. Few look classy, act classy, and they aren't classy. No generation, in American history, has been so totally void of class. The real tragedy is that few understand or know class when they see it and thus it gets farther and farther away. It may soon disappear completely. It's not just the way people dress, that's an arguable thing that's futile to discuss, especially with the young. Its the way people act that is eroding the fiber from the American cloth.

Nothing in life should be hid. It is a dangerous habit to refuse to confront reality or pretend that certain things do not happen. Or, that life does not have its darker sides, horrors, and perversions. But these acknowledgements can be personal and private. To imitate sophistication by publicly proclaiming that body waste stinks does not diminish the smell.

Examples of this void in class:

To have a President, when confronted with the most despicable act committed against a nation in modern times (when Iran took hostages from the American embassy in Tebran) proclaim that he was putting Christmas trees on the White House lawn to commemorate their captivity is an act so banal as to permanently scar the national senses;

To have a President declare, "I'm not a crook!"

To have a President hold up a hound dog by his ears, then pull up his shirt and show a long gash down his belly from a recent operation;

To have religion turned into a sideshow by television evangelists;

To have the National Endowment for the Arts fund an exhibit that shows a photograph of one man urinating into the mouth of another man in the name of art;

To have a paper like the *Wall Street Journal* report that oil companies were reaping such vast profits that one oil magnate was a little giddy when discussing the gushers of money swelling the company vaults;

To have two well-dressed assailants attack the CBS evening news anchor, while they kept asking him, "What is the frequency, Kenneth?" and to have the total national ink and electronic industry completely uncurious as to such a strange and phenomenal occurrence, when usually such an incident, with a lesser mortal, would have sent investigative ink and electronic tradesmen out in frenzied swarms;

To have nationally recognizable personalities tout health insurance to senior citizens on television; insurance that has absolutely no value;

To have a Jewish couple shamefully use the ruse of an ailing baby to coerce the Russian government to allow then to leave the Soviet Union without the ink and electronic tradesmen giving a notice after they had spent months raving and ranting about how terrible the Russians were to hold a sick baby hostage;

How crass and shameless can a nation become?

If someone wanted to do an analysis on American society they would but need to look at hair over the last few decades. Hair has mirrored the mood of the country perfectly. In the Fifties, there was the crew cut, everything neat and ordinary. Then came the Sixties and hair went completely wild, reflecting the "everyone doing their own thing." Then in the Seventies there was a sort of bland, not sure which way to go, and hair styles were more or less — wear it the way you like it. Then came the Eighties and the frizzled and frantic look. Nothing could more personify the Eighties than the frenzied, panic look.

The interesting thing about the trends of the last few years with women dressing in men's clothing and wearing their hair cut like men, and men wearing their hair more like women (The men's ponytail is expected to be the mod of the Nineties.) has not resulted in the sexes becoming more androgynous. What has happened is the law of opposites has taken control. Women are becoming more and more masculine and men are becoming more and more feminine. Based on the law of opposites, if this trend continues, women may well become the dominate sex in the Twenty-first Century.

It really began with Elvis Presley. Here was a dirt-pore, rural, small town Southerner who came from a crumpled, felt hat, tight lipped, narrow-eyed background, who suddenly had money and fame beyond understanding. With the same native shrewdness that characterizes many people from the wrong side of the track who suddenly make it, Elvis proceeded to transfer his taste and habits on the sons and daughters of the people who earlier had laughed at him and called him, "White trash!" Once Elvis made the state of one's hair a "statement," hair would never be the same. What had once been a woman's crowning glory was now something that could be used for sex, politics, religion, etc.

Elvis also invented nilly-slouch. This persona is one of a pouched, curled lip; a slothful attitude that radiates an aura that demands the subservience of everyone else without any reciprocal personal involvement. But, the single and most malignant seed of nilly-slouch, is that you can do anything you want and make the biggest mess possible, and its everyone else's responsibility to come along and clean it up.

These are nothing more than infantile attitudes and would be expected to gain wide acceptance from a young population who like to dream of when they were babies and had everything done for them. Babies and kids do not like authority and responsibility which makes nilly-slouch a mental opium.

This was why Elvis had such an appeal to women. Women saw in Elvis a grown baby upon whom they could infer a mother's love. At the same time, he had a man's body that could return that love with adult sex. This was a really potent combination. It would provide an endless source for fantasies. Elvis was Oedipus in morphosis.

The amazing thing about Elvis was that he not only appealed to the young and older women, he left his mark on a whole generation of older men. A vast segment of middle-aged men still have Dorian Grey images of Elvis in their psyches that manifest themselves in sideburns, turned up collars, and a certain swagger in their walk, and a slurred speech pattern. During any twenty-four hour period, thousands of middle-aged Elvis pretenders swagger in and out of truck stops throughout the country.

He was also a worldwide phenomenon. He influenced music, dress, and worse — attitudes — around the world. The Beatles would say that he was their musical inchoation. They would extend the nilly-slouch to the outer limits that would embrace drugs and religious cults. The seed of Elvis's persona would eventually achieve full growth and be clones in a strange and exotic body — at once male and female, almost neuter — Michael Jackson.

Here would come a diminutive cockalorum who thrills a generation by wearing one glove on one hand held out like Dr. Strangelove; struts backward on a stage squeaking over and over and over again, "I'm Bad! I'm Bad! I'm Bad!" and is considered an example for the youth of the world. Yet here is a gynandromorph who covets to own the bones of a sad, English freak called the Elephant Man.

The President of the United States, Ronald Wilson Reagan, honored Michael Jackson at a ceremony at the White House. Class?

From the President on down, its been a long time since there has been any demonstrative examples of genuine class. Actors, musicians, artists, engineers, truck drivers, waitresses, doctors, pilots, etc., etc., — the nilly-slouch is the contemporary addiction. A nation without class will end quicker than a nation without food. A nation must stand for something and that something must be something that elevates the human spirit and challenges the mind. Not only are the young no longer challenged in any meaningful way, they are daily subjected to political, educational, and religious leaders, at every level of society; wringing their hands, sobbing that all is hopeless — the drugs, the crime, the national debt, AIDS, abortion, etc. No wonder so many young people are on drugs and alcohol. If they watch a week of television its likely they will cringe from reality. Not only are the young people effected, but most adult Americans are retreating to any refuge that can provide some temporary peace and tranquility.

The terms couch potato and cocooning have recently come into usage to mean, "retreat from and shut out reality".

Benjamin J. Stein, a lawyer and economist, writing in the Los Angeles Times stated, "We are walled up in our houses, in our cars, in our persons, away from mobility, from good sounds, from each other. Don't wait for the new Dark Ages any longer. They're here."

SPIRIT

He replied, "Go your way, Daniel, because the words are closed up and sealed until the time of the end. Many will be purified, made spotless and refined, but the wicked will continue to be wicked. None of the wicked will understand, but those who are wise will understand."

Daniel 12:9

If humans could evolve through evolution and natural selection as the scientists claim that they can prove happened. If this is true and humans could grow and append to themselves that which was necessary to survive. Why then could they not develop a soul to survive death? Surely the latter would be no more difficult than the former.

In life there are a few rare moments when an almost eerie silence descends and time and motion seems to be suddenly suspended. It is in these very rare moments, that all humans have experienced at one time or the other, that the essence of spirituality can be breathed into the soul. Its a sobering and thought provoking experience whose impact remains long after the moment has evaporated regardless of the circumstances in which it occurs. No known pleasure of the flesh can, under any stimulance, come close to recreating this strange, mystic feeling.

Humans are totally enshroud with beauty so profound as to intoxicate the senses. This is true in the worst slums and hovels on earth as it is in the grandest palaces. Circumstances can place humans in slums, but only humans can put slums in humans. There are as many princes of government, industry, and science with slums in their hearts as there are in the hearts of poverty stricken residents of ghettos. The prophets of this planets have graced the spirit with magnificence, not from positions of wealth and comfort but from abject poverty. Some of the most beautiful plants on earth grow in swamps.

The hands that sculptured the planets and stars and whose brush mixed the colors of it all, fixed the standard for artistic beauty forever. The art contained in the museums of the world are only imitations of the real thing. The deftness of the petal of a white rose is so grand in execution that it tears the eye to view it. There are masterpieces right outside the doors of every dwelling in every ghetto on earth, that so surpass the works of Michelangelo, Rembrandt, and Matisse, that they pale in comparison. The great artists of every century have suffered in spirit and soul knowing that they could only imitate, never create. The ones who achieved the greatest success were the ones who died trying.

The deceitful, pseudo-intellectuals of the earth wring their hands and shake their fists at the heavens and cry, "No! No! No! There is nothing but me. Me! Me! Me!" Their own words clearly reflect who they really are.

Motion and its rhythms perform the world's greatest ballets. The surf twirling in tiny ripples, whirling around in roiling tunnels of blue and white dance nimbly upon stages of sand amid an ocean melody, cause even the greatest ballerina to blush with envy.

Bright colored leaves of every hue delicately balanced in an Autumn wind create airy canvases that warm the heart with just a moment's view.

The lowest humans, in the worst of circumstances, can

touch the most distant star or hold all creation in the palm of their vision, by opening the lens of their mind. More beauty has come from prison cells, than from princely palaces. There is no place under heaven that you can stand, if you could look far enough, that you could not see light. To those who seek spiritual truth, this is a holy revelation — there is light looking back, there is light to see now, and there is light looking ahead. *The only darkness there is, is when we fail to look in any direction at all.* If we fail to see beauty, its because we fail to see light. Its like the poet Wallace Stevens wrote:

"Beauty is momentary in the mind —
The fitful tracing of a portal;
But in the flesh it is immortal."

To learn to live in harmony and expand and grow, humans need to look at the world around them. Everything within the universe expands and grows by giving. Oceans live and throb fed from the blood of tiny veins of waters from across the surface of the earth. Trees that reach up to the sky feed from minerals beneath the ground and the sunlight and rain from the sky above. Flowers trade nectar to bees for pollen like comets feed new stars and new stars are seeds for new universes. Humans represent the only greed in the universe. Humans are the only organisms in the entire universe that are wantonly avaricious. Humans can only receive if they give, and if they give, its never possible to receive all that's given in return.

Its easy to see how humans find the simple rules of the universe almost impossible to discern when they alone ravish the earth night and day to live beyond not only what is necessary, but even beyond what is normal. Animals that walk the land; plants that grow from the soil; birds that fly in the sky; fish that swim in the rivers and seas; trees, oil, gas, and coal for fuel; waters from rivers, streams, oceans, and from the sky for drinking; and minerals of all kinds for manufacturing and for adornment; even the dirt for building materials; salt for seasoning; and fibers for clothing — humans ravage insatiably like sharks eternally feeding on everything in their paths. It is natural and normal for all organisms to survive by feeding upon specific prey(s), whether the prey is animal, mineral, or vegetable. It is not natural or normal for any organism to feed for the joy of feeding or to feed wantonly and avariciously. Almost every human physical problem can be traced directly or indirectly to excess. Humans eat to much, drink to much, smoke to much, take to many drugs, exercise to much, work to much, are sexually promiscuous, argue to much, are to violent; its endless.

There are approximately 5,000,000,000 humans residing on earth at the present time. Most of these humans live in large urban areas where life is lived at maximum stress. Why? If this were asked of the scientists who monitor and track populations, the answer that would most often be given would be, "They come here looking for a better life." Try to imagine a life in any rural spot upon the face of the earth including Ethiopia and Antarctic that could possibly be worse than the hell raked drug, crime, squalor, and AIDS infested streets in most major cities of the world. No! They come for greed. Few of the teeming millions that flock to the cities of the world work hard for better education, homes and food. They work for televisions, radios, gold chains, fancy tennis shoes, watches, leather and plastic clothing, and cars. They seek not a better life but a life filled with material things.

On Sunday, July 23, 1989, at 2:58 a.m., in a crack house in Washington, D.C., 13-year-old Derrick Conner was gunned down. Police sources said the youth was working as a runner for a drug dealer. This was reported in *The Washing-*

ton Post on Wednesday, July 26, 1989. The young man was described as a natural leader who wrote poetry. An advisor who had worked with Derrick in a mentor program stated, "Derrick was a person mesmerized by materialism."

One of the last times Derrick's father, Kenneth Davis, saw him he noticed Derrick was wearing $150.00 tennis shoes.

A niece, from Trinidad, remarked after her uncle was the victim of a racist attack after he turned down the wrong street in New York City, "I'm going home. The only thing nice about New York is the money."

There are two great problems that strike at the very heart of social conditions the world over. They are not new. They are as old as society itself. These conditions are political "causes" and "sports." These two problems are so alike and so connected that they have to be linked together to be able to see the signifance of their grip on society and why. Politicians (government leaders) must have a cause that is of great concern to the majority of citizens, or they must develop a cause and convince a majority of the citizens that it is a matter of the greatest urgency. Israeli leaders successfully used foreign gods for centuries as causes. Roman leaders used Christians and Huns among others as causes for rallying the people. Hitler used the Jews and southern political leaders for decades used the Negroes. In recent time many leaders like Fidel Castro and Ayatollah Khomeini and others have successfully used the United States as causes. The idea is simple, if you can get the majority of the people intensely focused on some issue, especially if its an emotional or nationalistic one, then it will blot out the real problems that are besetting that society.

It really amounts to political slight-of-hand. To understand the real problems of society it is necessary to forget the political right hand and focus on the left one. At the present time, drugs are being touted as the number one issue in America. The amount of ink and electronic attention being focused on this one human frailty is enormous. It is a significant problem; it is not the major problem in America or the world today. The major problems in America and the world today are: ***ignorance and greed***. Private family farms are systematically being eliminated in America today. If Americans think hospital and medical cost are expensive now since the corporations took over medicine, wait until they see the food cost once the corporations finish taking over the growing of food. Only an ignorant people would pay three times as much for gasoline as they once did and then pump the gas themselves. Only an ignorant people would pay four times the cost of a hamburger, wait on themselves and then clean off the table afterward. Only an ignorant people would elect humans to critical public offices who have known criminal records. Only an ignorant people would send 1.2 million dollars a day to television evangelists who dress like Elvis Presley and preach like sideshow barkers or carnival shills. Only an ignorant people would drink 5.2 million dollars worth of sweetened water every day. Only an ignorant people would smoke 1.3 billion cigarettes a day while 356 humans are dying each day from lung cancer. Only a wanton, avaricious people could produce 1.2 trillion pounds of garbage and trash every day.

Humans participate in sports because it offers the opportunity to become better at something than anyone else in the eyes of the vast majority of the population. Sports are one of the few paying endeavors that requires no ancestral pedigree to enter. Most sports icons come from very meager and obscure circumstances. Except for polo, golf, tennis, and sailboating, it is rare to see anyone of privileged background reach the pinnacle of any sport. This has been true down through history. It is also the accepted human endeavor for transference of and sharing glory. If a soccer, football, baseball, etc. team representing a community, city, state, country, or organization wins a championship game, all of the humans that make up those entities share in the glory and transference with, "We won." A sports fan reaps great ephemeral rewards with a minimum investment of money and little if any investment of mental or physical effort. *Sports are the metaphysical placebos for the masses.*

There is in scientific positivism the concept of *"argument from silence"* the belief that if something has not been found, it cannot have existed in significant quantities. It is virtually impossible to prove absence. This comes from *Black Athena: The Afroasiatic Roots of Classical Civilization, Volume I: The Fabrication of Ancient Greece, 1785-1985,* by Martin Bernal. When scientists set the rules, the rules always favor the scientists. With three words — argument from silence — they can exclude, in their own minds and industry, all serious academic discourt or consideration of religion or paranormal phenomena. This does not eliminate, the scientific industry not withstanding, proof that there are religious truths. Truths that transcend reality require faith. A Mr. Simon Brown was quoted in *The Wall Street Journal,* relative to some strange circles that were appearing in farm fields in a section of England near the Stonehenge monuments. (This was after a variety of experts and scientists could not find a viable answer.) "It means we have absolutely no bloody idea of what goes on around us. It's one of those eternal mysteries. Long may they continue." Said Mr. Brown, sagely.

Scientists and academicians argue (as a reason for being reluctant to "get into religion") that more people have been killed in the name of God by religious zealots than by any other force on earth. What they apply here is the "argument from silence." The silent part is that the number of people that have been killed by religious zealots over the centuries is infinitesimal compared to the millions upon millions of people that have been killed and are continuing to be killed every day by the weapons and tools of war that were created by the scientists themselves. Shifting blame is a historic rouse for burying personal guilt and responsibility. Its never been a very good cover.

The scientists and academicians are more than willing to accept this kind of money. They even fight over money for researching and developing new and better ways to kill more and more people. Yet, in the most fragrant acts of casuistry, they feign horror at the thought of even discussing, let alone, giving any credence to a religious philosophy that might have as its only goal — peace and love in the country. These scientists and academicians are not just cynics; they are insidious cynics, smiling wanly in the sunlight but are jackals who feed on human and animal carcasses in the darkness.

Scientists and academicians are not against religion because they think its a myth. They think its a myth because they are against it.

Faith exists at many levels and has many characteristics. Faith is absolutely essential for peace of mind whether a human is religious, nonreligious, or atheistic. Faith is incorrectly presumed to be a mental, mechanical affirmation of confidence in a known probability. Mental, mechanical affirmation is trusting that an elevator will go up and down without falling or an airplane will reach its destination without crashing. None of this is faith, *mental, mechanical affirmation is trust, not faith.*

Faith is the affirmation that something exists or will exist even though it may never be seen. Faith requires vision, trust does not. The biblical stories of the founding of Israel, demonstrate magnificent faith by the Jewish patriarchs. These patriarchs had faith that ultimately God would fulfill his promise of giving the Hebrews a land of milk and honey, even though they personally, almost without exception, would never see it themselves, and it would be hundreds or even scores of years beyond their lives that it would occur. It is when one can read the entire scope of these promises by God, as revealed in holy text, that the grandeur of this faith can be seen.

Military personnel and espionage agents who fight for country and honor (not mercenaries and traitors) are required to have more faith than any religious leader. They go forth knowing little more than that there is a great chance that they will be killed. What they have to have above all else is the faith that regardless of the outcome as to their living or dying, is that their personal beliefs will be sustained — that their country will ultimately be victorious and will continue to survive and prosper and that their close relatives and friends will be safe.

Exceptional leaders must have faith beyond human understanding. Abraham Lincoln was such a leader. During the darker moments of the struggle during the Civil War, in his depressive state, doubts would creep in, but only temporarily, for he never doubted the ultimate outcome. All his life he demonstrated this almost mystic ability of knowing the ultimate outcome of events. It was the thing that sustained him throughout his life.

There is no power in the universe equal to faith — not nuclear, not hydrogen, not magnetic, not gravity, not anything. Whatever can be conceived through vision can be achieved with faith in time. It may not be achieved in one lifetime or a thousand lifetimes, but if the faith is maintained, *it will be achieved.*

Words cannot adequately relate the mystery of what this

means in terms of what is possible to those who understand and can grasp the true dimensions of faith. One can dedicate their life to a small segment of a big dream with total confidence that someday that dream will be a reality. The irony is that we are all part of a bigger dream whether we acknowledge it or not. We are part of a heavenly dream moving in a heavenly draft. The difference between those of faith and the faithless, is that those of faith are aware of the journey and enjoy the trip. The faithless neither enjoy the trip or are aware of the journey.

We perish without faith and vision.

Monks in the dark ages labored lifetimes copying holy scriptures realizing that they would not finish but with vision and faith that others would continue the work. They also had the vision and faith that regardless of future wars, famines, floods, fires, and natural disasters these manuscripts would survive and they did. How enriched the world is today because of their vision and faith.

A wise man once remarked, "Humans are always squeezing out the gnat while they're swallowing the camel." At any given moment of time, twenty-four hours a day, three-hundred and sixty-five days a year, year-in-and-year-out, people of all races, on every continent of the world, in every city of the world, and in most of the dwellings places on this planet, there are millions of humans who take no role whatsoever in government or social concerns beyond being self-appointed critics. Less than ten percent of the world's population has any participatory role in any form of activity that contributes to the welfare of society in general. The true miracle of life is that it has the eternal elasticity to contract and expand to absorb the constant shock of human folly without self-destructing. Unlike all other animals on this planet, few humans ever reach maturity, either mentally or emotionally.

The primary reason for this is that it has always been easier for leaders to control their constituents by making them dependent rather than making them responsible. A responsible human needs very little government support. A comedian once had a favorite line that he would shout, "What are the preachers gonna do when the Devil is saved?" If just thirty percent of the earth's population were to mature tomorrow and become responsible humans, half the required public services such as police, fire, hospitals, military, and the hundreds of supporting ancillary services would not be needed.

It has long been evident to police officers, ministers, school teachers, counselors of all kinds, judges, politicians, and journalists, that ninety-eight percent of human problems that they see, hear, and have to be involved in every day, are simple and petty. Only two percent are major. Even countries become involved in disputes that erupt into major confrontations over mundane and petty things. By far the vast majority of conflicts (ninety-five percent) have to do with possession in one form or the other and often over something insignificant when viewed from a point of maturity within the whole context of the universe.

To prove this point just hand a baby anything from a string to an acorn and then try to take it away. Greed, next to sex, is the most tactile of human emotions. Greed is bad enough when it has to do with tangible possessions, but it is both comic and tragic when it involves, as it most often does, intangible things. It is breathtaking to see the intangible and clearly undefined things that most humans believe that they personally possess and covet and are willing to engage, verbally and often violently, anyone who transgresses them. Many believe that they own certain portions of public thoroughfares. As clearly impossible as it would be to assign certain spaces of Expressways, there are those who have killed and wounded perceived trespassers into their portion of a chimerical express lane.

There are hundreds of these chimeric possessions. Express lanes in supermarkets, counter spaces at restaurants, seats on public and private transportation conveyances, parking places, seats in any facility public or private (including religious institutions); the list is endless.

There are millions who are offended by anyone looking at them, or looking at someone who is with them. In many places throughout the world, it can be extremely dangerous to even glance at a stranger.

Humans around the earth are killed and maimed every minute of the day because of disagreements over television and radio programs, over the title of a song, over which sports or entertainment figure is the best.

If every human is treating everyone the way they want to be treated, masochism is epidemic. This is especially true in New York City and Washington, D.C.

Humans refuse to mature. They refuse to put away childish behavior. The irresponsible humans crawling upon the surface of the earth are like legions of gnats. They do nothing but irritate and aggravate.

These immature humans have kalaidecopic thought patterns. Everything is seen as if through a lens, shades and colors and patterns interweave and mesh, ever moving back and forth but never coalescing into concrete and definitive images, visions, and hopes. They are forever viewing all creation through misty lens, never seeing the sunshine just above the mist — always conforming, never being transformed by taking that tiny first step forward to stand alone.

Intelligence and maturity have nothing whatsoever to do with professional educational training. To be transformed, humans need wisdom and wisdom comes on the winds from heaven. Heavenly winds that are a gift available to all.

Being smart, being intelligent, or being bright, in human terms, have nothing to do with wisdom. Intelligence and being smart have to do with progressive assimilation of details and experiences in order to formulate accepted or logical conclusions or actions. Almost any animal can be trained to act intelligent, within human context.

Wisdom, like true talent, is a gift. Like a talent, wisdom has to be used and nourished to retain it. Wisdom is the ability to discern reality on both a tangible and intangible level. A great prophet once spoke most majestically, relative to wisdom's very heart when he said, "Judge not appearance, but judge righteous judgment."

The solution to all problems new and old the world over requires wisdom, not intelligence. Intelligent participants have applied human thoughts over this century that have not only provided no solutions, but have in most cases made the situation worse. They have only placed patches on the innertube of the earth so many times that there are few places left that can be patched. What is needed is a completely new tube.

Some of the most childish behavior found within the universe is found in the halls of academia. Intelligence and maturity have nothing whatsoever to do with leadership or position. Political and industrial leaders the earth over are administering in circumstances of chance and chaos in general and with pathos and legerdemain more common.

Wisdom is always rejected by the greedy and immature, because wisdom always emanates from an unselfish and unbiased position. Wisdom is not possible from a parochial point of view. The very heart of wisdom is that it flows from a new and fresh spring of pure water.

If a leader of wisdom could come forth today, wisdom

could resolve some ancient and terrible conflagrations that have continued to rage down through the centuries.

Jews and Arabs born of the same seed have lived together in the same land in hatred for thousands of years; since they will continue to live in the same land together thousands of years more, why not live it in peace? Two semitic peoples of such rich and lavish cultures could, living together in peace, provide untold treasures to an impoverished world. If you share the same house, everyone must cook the food; for if its true that, "They that eat my bread also sing my songs." Then its equally true that if the song is not liked, it may be sung, but out of tune. The sound is then unpleasant for all to hear. A plot of ground with a ripe fig tree is better than a plot of earth full of briars.

Prejudice is a universal disorder. It is practiced against Africans more than any other race. The African race is a race apart. The inherent culture of the African is more opposite when placed against another culture than any other on earth. It is this acute difference, that makes the prejudice so different. On every continent of the earth, including their own, the African, once exposed to another culture, attempts to practice that culture and abandon their own. This has been true from the days the Ethiopians adopted Judaism, the Africans adopted the mores of the colonial Europeans, and the worse case of all, when the African slaves in the South, before the Civil War, adopted the habits and manners of their masters. With few exceptions, the Africans have had very poor role models. *If the Africans cannot accept themselves as they really are, then no one else will either.*

It is truth not ignorance that provokes the most fear. Most humans fear most humans. It is the truth of our own nature that provides the fear we have of others. The more uncomfortable we are with our own nature, the more uncomfortable we are with other people's nature. *The happiest and most trusted people on earth are the people who are most trustworthy and comfortable with themselves.* To change others we must first change ourselves.

Criminals should be treated as they treat each other. The death penalty is strictly enforced and several prisoners each year are executed in every prison in the world. There is no prison on earth where there is no death penalty. It exist in every prison, in every country. There is no preliminary hearing, no trial, no appeal, and no appeal for clemency is allowed. Death is swift, usually a homemade knife or ice pick to the heart. Rarely is the death penalty invoked because of a murder. Criminals in prison invoke the death penalty for those they presume to be traitors, the theft of cigarette(s), passion among competing prisoners, and a misunderstood glance. *If criminals believe that the theft of a cigarette or a glance that can't be absolutely understood is worthy of death without trial or appeal, why then should they object to the death penalty being invoked for the brutal slaying of innocent people?* Humans live by the rules they believe in, they also die by the same rules.

Addiction is a self inflicted wound. Like all wounds it may be healed, depending on how wide and how deep it is, by stitching it up cleanly, or cauterizing it with a source of heat, or leaving it open where it will continue to bleed and fester until it brings death. Except in extremely rare circumstance, addiction will not heal itself. It requires immediate and continued attention, either by the human that has the addiction or by a professional who understands the nature of the addiction. There are no good, bad, better, or worse addictions — food, money, gambling, drugs, alcohol, tobacco, sex — when addictive, all addiction is fatal if not curbed. The addiction that does not consume the body consumes the soul. Addiction is not caused by lack of will, it is caused by lack of faith. *No one can be what they can not imagine themselves to be*. Faith has the power to steady and steel the most unsteady mind trying to flee from a strangling addictive demon.

A view of life in its entirety is essential to understand life at any level. Birth, life, death, God, all must be seen as a whole not as a part. To think that understanding life in its wholeness can be understood by viewing it piece-by-piece is like trying to visualize a seashore by examining one, single grain of sand. Everything in the universe was created whole not in part.

The earth can be placed in the palm of your hand. Its really a very small planet. Its mainly water, mountains, and trees. At any given time a variety of wind patterns gently or violently sweep about to and fro causing clouds to form or disperse and rain and snow to fall. Half of the earth is in sunlight while the other half is in darkness. When viewed as a whole, everyone lives on an island. Every land mass is surrounded by water and waves gently rock back and forth on sandy shores or break violently against crags and cliffs. Streams flow into rivers and rivers flow into the oceans. There are cities on the sea, in the mountains, and on the plains. There are great metropolitan areas and small villages. People are constantly being born in straw huts and gleaming hospitals. Death is as common and frequent as sunlight. Some sleep while some work. Everything alive on the earth in your hand at every single instance of history occupies some space — a mother's womb, a deep diamond mine, a skyscraper, a hospital bed, a prison cot, a field of corn, a battlefield bunker, a lover's arm, a wrecked automobile, millions of people, millions of places. They speak in many tongues and have a variety of skin colors, but they are more alike than they are different. They all need the same substances to live. There is no monopoly anywhere upon the earth you hold in your hand for honesty, religiosity, ignorance, poverty, wealth, wisdom, and greed. All human virtues and vices are spread fairly equally about the earth. Surely its plainly seen when viewed from this perspective that happiness and greed is universal and shared equally by all. When viewing this great panorama of life, its easy to see that true pleasure and happiness has nothing whatsoever to do with a person's material condition, it has only to do with their inner condition. The warriors in Africa and the Indians in the Amazon laugh as much as the condo dwellers on Fifth Avenue or the parvenu on the Champs Elysees.

Humans viewed in total are all confronted with exactly the same problems. Riches and hygiene does not remove worry, disease, fear, and death. Poverty and squaller do not prevent happiness and fulfillment. A trillionaire with AIDS or cancer is as helpless as the starving man in Ethiopia. Death is truly an equal opportunity employer. While the healthy, migrant farm worker is richer still than the internationally famous rock star or Hollywood starlet who are on drugs, alcohol, and need pills to sleep, pills to wake up, and pills to keep going and who are never really cognizant of reality.

This is easy to see when watching all of it take place at the same time on the earth in the palm of your hand. It can be easily seen that the wise of the earth realize value before lost. Because it is most often that humans only realize value after something has been lost. When legs are lost the pleasure of walking is suddenly realized. The lost of sight reminds of how beautiful the world is. The lost of a loved one reminds of all the things that should have been done and said that were not.

It all comes down to faith. Faith is absolute to life. Without faith there is no life. Its the core of existence. All things are possible with faith. Nothing is possible without faith. Without faith there is no vision. Without vision there is no hope. Without hope there is nothing. If one looks back as far as history is recorded there can clearly be seen a pattern. True progress has not been made in the human condition. The things that would result in progress are ignored over and over again, century-after-century by all the world over. Intelligence is scorned and even feared. Crime ebbs and peaks but never slackens. Wars are fought over and over again. Disputes continue beyond the point of sanity. The Middle East at this very moment is in generally the same condition as it was some 6000 years ago. The warring parties then are the warring parties now.

These disputes, like most others now and in the past, are over land and God. Many claim the same God, but recognize him in different forms and recognize his prophets as different beings. All seek God's favor and seek his security. When you hold the earth in your hand and view these conflicts taking place in different places around the planet, its plain to witness that the only partiality shown by God is the equal horror visited on both sides.

Where there has been victory claimed and God given the credit, its also been the case that what God gives, God takes away. The victories God has bestowed are equally offset by the defeats he has also given.

Progress cannot be counted if new diseases like AIDS develop as quick as new miracle medicines. Gas driven automobiles and atomic energy are not progress if they destroy the environment. Drugs that placate the mind do not represent progress if they foster dependency.

All life needs food, air, and water. Humans need one thing more — peace of mind. Most of the sorrow and horror of the earth since Adam and Eve have been caused by troubled minds. A human that has true peace of mind will cause no one any problem — neither themselves or others.

Every human, at some precise moment in their lives, decides to journey toward light or darkness. They make this decision both conscientiously and unconscientiously; they make it both willfully and unwillfully. They do make it themselves. When their journey comes to an end, they require no judgment as to which choice was made. Their final destination is their final judgment.

> ***As for humans, their days are as grass: as a flower of the field, so they flourisheth. For the wind passeth over it, and it is gone; and the place thereof shall know it no more.***
>
> ***Psalm 103: 15-16***

EPILOGUE

And God remembered Noah, and every living thing, and all the cattle that was with him in the ark: and God made a wind to pass over the earth, and the waters receded.

Genesis 8:1

Every object in the universe is constantly in motion moving toward or away from another object. Some objects, like humans, attract and some repel. All of this continuous motion and attraction and repulsion creates monumental oceans of energy whose waves eternally wash upon the planets and stars. Great surfs of energies race across the universe with stars delicately balancing upon their crests. Against the majesty of this heavenly sea, humans pale into insignificance without accepting the gift of existence with all its magnificent possibilities.

The great blessings of life are that regardless of storms, floods, famines, plagues, earthquakes, fires, and hundreds of other disasters that occur over and over again, afterward, over time, a gentle wind from heaven blows and things return to normal once more. This is why faith and wisdom are the keys to living life without fear and with peace of mind. All of the approximately 5,000,000,000 people now occupying this planet, did not exist for millions of years prior to their birth, and they will not exist after their death for millions of years. That small fraction of time sandwiched in between birth and death is so brief that it should be savored as a rare meal, rather than scattered recklessly like chaff in the wind.

Few people seem to have any sound rationality. If humans have a soul and the soul is eternal, then it existed before they were born and it will exist after they die. The thought of eternity causes strange and troubling feelings to descend on many as they contemplate such a limitless period of existence. This feeling is a result of contemplating this existence in human terms. To most humans the thought of existing for a few hours without assistance from alcohol or drugs, is viewed with great anxiety and horror. To such humans, there is no mystery as to why they view eternity with alarm.

One of the greatest thinkers the earth has produced once stated. "A good person has nothing to fear in life or death." This is a simple thought but carries the strength of eternity. To those who profess a spiritual and religious bent to their lives, it is somewhat puzzling exactly why they view eternity with such foreboding. Many young children and a few adults, at special moments in their lives, have an experience where the ecstasy of the moment's pleasure is so intense, that earthly time disappears. It is a rare and fragile moment. Once the moment dissolves, there is an acute feeling of wistfulness. People who have had "near death" experiences describe a similar feeling of euphoria and an overwhelming feeling of nostalgia when they return to their bodies.

The darkest satire that is inflicted against the human experience, is that body of intelligentsia, who pout at every human kindness and prattle and promenade at every human weakness. This has been most evident in the last several years in the rise and fall of a number of religious and political leaders. These human heartache scavengers have no interest in either religion or politics, or the truly good-hearted, faithful adherents who send in their money to these religious wretches, or the voters who place their trust in these wayward politicians. These human heartache scavengers are not motivated by their benevolence for the human race, but for the euphoric fix that these human foibles reinforced in their own minds that all life is just a sham.

There are many problems in life and there are equal numbers of opportunities. There are many good qualities and many bad qualities in things in general and certain humans specifically. There is no evil within the limitless space of the universe equal to hypocrisy. The poet Milton wrote, *"For neither human nor angel can discern hypocrisy, the only evil that walks invisibly."*

The fabric of human existence is rich in shallow diversities, but is richer in many deep and shared traits. There has been only one message that has been delivered down the expressways of time by Gods, prophets, philosophers, and divine teachers and it is simple: walk humble before creation and be loving, kind, and generous with all kindred creatures. Nothing truly harmful can ever befall a spirit that demonstrates these simple virtues.

> ***But the souls of the righteous are in the hand of God, and there shall no torment touch them.***
>
> ***In the sight of the unwise they seemed to die: and their departure is taken for misery,***
>
> ***And their going from us to be utter destruction: but they are in peace.***

For though they be punished in the sight of men, yet is their hope full of immortality.

And having been a little chastised, they shall be greatly rewarded: for God proved them, and found them worthy for himself.

The Wisdom of Solomon

— The Beginning —